Eaten Alive

by

Carnivorous Plants

Kathleen J. Honda
Makoto Honda

To Courtney

Venus flytrap

Published in 2015 in the United States of America.

Copyright © 2015 Kathleen J. Honda & Makoto Honda.
Book layout by Microsoft Publisher 2003.
Digital image processing by Nikon Capture NX.

ISBN-13: 978-1517124779
ISBN-10: 1517124778
Carnivorous Plants Juvenile Literature. Grades 2-4.

This book is available in Color edition, B&W edition and Kindle edition from Amazon.com
Visit: www.honda-e.com/ea.htm

Published by CreateSpace Independent Publishing Platform.
Printed and bound in the United States of America.

2020-May-20

CONTENTS

Cobra plant, northern California

Sundew and a bug

Chapter 1

Meat-Eating Plants

Did you remember to eat your veggies at dinner?

Besides producing oxygen that we breathe, plants are a very important food for us. We eat them everyday. There are many animals that rely on plants. If there were no plants, these animals would starve to death.

But did you know there are plants that eat animals?

Yes, some plants catch and eat insects and other small bugs for their meal.

Plants normally get all the nutrients they need from the soil they grow in. That's why we give fertilizer to the flower pot. That's their food.

There are places in the world where the soil is poor and does not contain enough nourishment for the plants to stay healthy. Swampy places and other types of wetlands are good examples of this.

Imagine that you are a plant and happen to be in one of these areas — you are hungry everyday because there isn't enough food in the soil. Animals can move around looking for food until they find some. But plants cannot move; they are stuck in the soil.

Venus flytrap,
North Carolina

A linear-leaved sundew plant in northern Michigan

In the long history of green flowering plants that are forced to live in these poor soils, some plants came up with an idea nobody had ever dreamt of — catch buzzing bugs and eat them!

After all, annoying bugs are everywhere. All you have to do is catch them.

These bug-catching plants are called "carnivorous" plants, which means meat-eating. There are more than 760 different kinds of meat-eating plants in the world. Some grow in bogs and swamps in North America; some grow in tropical jungles.

But how do they manage to catch such fast moving insects? If you have ever tried to catch a fly or other insect, you know how nimble they are. It's impossible to catch them.

The answer is, these meat-hungry plants use "tricks." Their leaves are modified into clever traps to catch unwary bugs. These traps are so colorful that insects mistake them for flowers that they are accustomed to visiting. The traps often lure bugs with sweet nectar, just like real flowers do. What bugs do not know is that these beautiful, colorful leaves might be their last stop — the bugs do not leave the plant. They are going to end up in the plant's stomach!

Thread-leaf sundews in bloom, the Florida Panhandle

There are four major trap types used by carnivorous plants: (a) **Snapping** like a bear trap, (b) **Sticky** glue like a flypaper, (c) **Slippery** pitfalls, and (d) **Sucking** up by a suction trap. Let's examine what kind of tricks each has in store for its prey.

Butterwort's flypaper trap

A wasp sipping pitcher plant's nectar

Chapter *2*

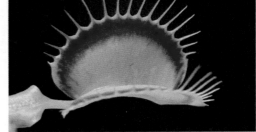

Venus Flytrap

A fly notices something red on the ground. A bright red color among the green grass. The fly comes closer to investigate. It's a small plant. The fly lands nearby.

The leaf is like a clamshell, two halves connected in the middle. There are stiff spines along the edges.

But it's not just the red color that is attractive. There's a band of nectar inside, just below the spines.

From the outside, the spine fence is in the way. The fly must enter between the V-shaped walls.

A little cautious at first, the fly starts to sip the nectar. It's so delicious!

A new trap leaf in the making

A Venus flytrap growing in the wild

As it enjoys the nectar, the fly touches a tiny hair in the middle of the leaf surface. The nectar is so tasty, the fly continues to lick, moving forward in the leaf. There is another tiny hair… The fly feels something is moving.

Oh, NO! The leaf is closing. Forgetting the nectar, the fly senses that he's in danger and tries to jump out.

It's too late. The leaf closes so swiftly, creating a cage of bars to prevent the escape. Before you know it, the fly is pinched between the two walls.

This is how the Venus flytrap hunts its

Trigger hairs on a
Venus flytrap leaf

meal.

The tiny hairs on the leaf turn out to be trigger hairs. The first time the fly touches one, nothing happens. Preoccupied with the nectar, the fly touches a hair again. The second touch signals the plant to trigger the trap. SNAP!

Indeed, the Venus flytrap is quietly counting how many times the trigger hairs are touched.

If an insect touches a hair the second time, there is a good chance that the insect has reached the middle of the trap and cannot easily escape. Very clever, don't you think?

Two days later ...

15

The trigger hairs grow in the middle of the leaf — usually three on each wall. As an insect sips nectar just below the spines, a large insect will surely brush a trigger hair. But a tiny bug, say, shorter than a quarter of an inch, may not touch any hairs at all.

It takes a lot of energy for a small plant to close the trap, so the Venus flytrap only goes after a large meal worth its time and effort.

When the trap does snap, there are some small gaps between the spines, and a small, unworthy bug has a second chance to sneak out. But big spiders and flies cannot leave.

A trapped bug moves around in a panic inside the closed leaf, touching the sensitive trigger hairs again and again and again.

Venus flytrap
with a spider

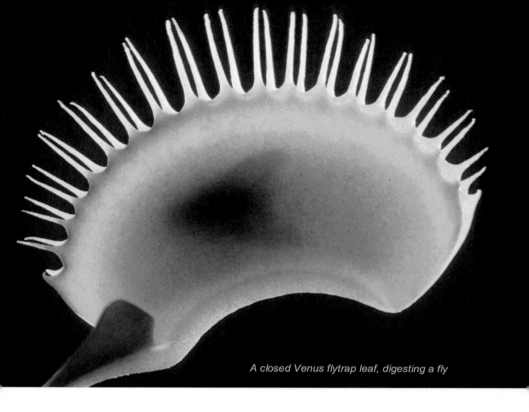

A closed Venus flytrap leaf, digesting a fly

This really excites the plant because it's a sure sign something big and "alive" has been captured. The leaf continues to tighten its grip, closing the clamshell trap more firmly. Often, the pressure is so strong, the captured prey is crushed between the two walls.

Eventually — in a few hours — the trap starts to pour digestive juices. This will suffocate the unlucky prey if it is still alive. In this closed trap, the prey is broken down in the digestive fluids, just like food is broken down in your stomach. The trap remains closed while the plant absorbs this delicious bug soup. This will last for a week to ten days.

After all the nutrients are absorbed, the trap opens slowly. Inside is the dry skeleton of the victim. The wind and rain will clean the dinner table for the next meal to come by. One leaf can eat an insect meal probably three times at most.

If you want to *trick* the Venus flytrap, touch any trigger hair twice — the same one or different ones — within 20 seconds. The trap will snap shut. But it will open the next

Venus flytraps in the wild

day because the plant does not find any food. You can fool a trap about ten times before it stops closing.

The Venus flytrap produces white flowers in the spring. Do you think anyone

Venus flytrap flowers

would know that these innocent-looking, delicate flowers belong to this deadly, meat-eating plant?

The tall flower stem keeps pollinators away from the danger of hungry traps on the ground. Venus flytraps don't want to eat bees and other pollinators because the pollinators

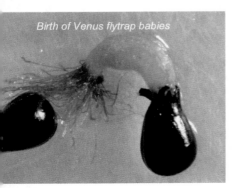
Birth of Venus flytrap babies

are very important for the plants in order to make seeds.

19

Dewy sundew leaves, Oregon

Chapter 3

Sticky Flypaper

Sundews are another type of insect-eating plant. They use sticky glue to trap their small animal prey.

If you happen to be in a bog or where the soil is moist, you may notice small plants with dewy leaves. Sundew leaves look like jewelry that glitters in the sun.

When sundews cover a large field in a

Sundews growing in northern California

meadow, they create a red carpet that is sprinkled with thousands of diamonds.

Flying insects may be attracted to these shiny dews. Curious, a fly decides to take a closer look.

That is a big mistake. The moment it lands on a sundew leaf, the legs of the fly are mired down in the sticky glue.

It's a trap! But it's too late for the fly. The more it struggles to free itself, the more

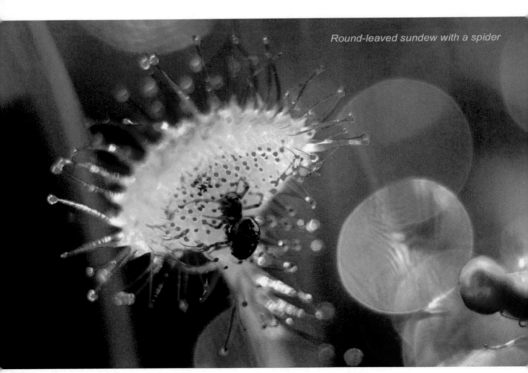
Round-leaved sundew with a spider

Sundew savoring a tasty fly

it's entangled in the nasty glue.

The surface of the sundew leaf is covered with hundreds of tiny hairs, called "tentacles." Each tentacle has a crystal-clear droplet of dew at the tip. What bugs do not know is that these shiny dews are a deadly and powerful glue which can catch anything that lands on them.

The struggle of the insect sends a signal to nearby tentacles and they too begin to flex toward the prey — like the deadly tentacles of an enormous octopus. The tentacles slowly push the prey to the center of the leaf. For a large insect, the entire leaf wraps around the victim's body. Often, the glue

Sundew tentacles with a sticky droplet

covers the entire prey. This will suffocate the poor insect.

Gradually, the sticky glue switches to digestive juices. The insect body begins to break down, creating a melting insect stew. The sundew leaf absorbs the delicious meal. This gives the plant vital nourishment. Often, after the plant finishes the meal, only a small, hard shell of the insect remains on the leaf.

5 min.

10 min.

15 min.

20 min.

25

Round-leaved sundew with a damselfly

Sundew leaves are usually small and can only catch a fly or a mosquito, but some sundews have leaves several inches or longer. These sundews will capture larger insects such as crane flies, dragon-flies and butterflies. Sometimes these sundews resemble a Christmas tree with all sorts of

26

insects stuck on the leaves.

In the wild, many sundews often grow together covering a large, moist field. Big insects may be captured by the cooperation of neighbors, each enjoying its share of the catch.

A crane fly falling victim to the English sundew

Sticky glue on a butterwort leaf

Sundews are not the only plants with the idea of catching bugs with glue. Butterworts are another.

Many butterworts produce attractive flowers in the spring. The tall flower stem supports a nodding, colorful flower of yellow, purple and white.

But don't be fooled by their showy blossoms. Their leaves are dangerous traps for small winged insects.

Butterwort rosettes

Yellow-flowered butterworts blooming in the Florida Panhandle

Butterworts produce green leaves lying flat on the ground. If you touch the leaf, it feels like melting butter. This explains the butterwort name. If you use a magnifying glass, you can see tiny hairs on the leaf surface with a dew-like droplet at the tip. These are glues to catch tiny insects, just like the glues on the sundew leaves.

Soon after a bug is captured, the leaf starts to produce digestive juices. The prey is broken down in the liquid and the nutrients are quickly absorbed through the leaf surface in a matter of hours.

Purple-flowered butterwort, Michigan

A gnat landed on a butterwort's sticky leaf

A butterwort flower
and a syrphid fly

31

Chapter *4*

*S*lippery Pitfall

In the American Southeast, there are vast stretches of grassland, with some tall pine trees. They are called savannas. The grass-covered ground is always moist and acidic.

Pitcher plants growing in Alabama

This is home to eight different kinds of pitcher plants, another type of carnivorous plant. Pitcher plants use their leaves as a pitfall trap to catch many bugs flying and crawling. The leaves of the pitcher plants hold water inside, like a pitcher.

Pitcher plant blossoms

These plants produce colorful flowers in the spring. Usually, the flowers bloom before the new spring pitcher leaves, so that insects pollinating the flowers do not have to worry about being captured by the pitfall trap.

Pitchers grow from the ground, like trumpets sticking out of the grass. They come in various sizes. Some grow to three feet high. Pitchers are often brilliantly colored to lure insects. Bees and flies mistake them for flowers and land on them.

But it is not just vibrant colors that attract insects. There is sweet nectar on the pitcher.

Pitcher plant colony in Florida

The pitcher has a lid at the top. The lid does not move. This is where the nectar is most plentiful. But this is a lure.

For flying insects, the lid is a convenient landing pad. But the under-surface is lined with tiny, downward-pointing hairs, and it is very slippery. Busy with the delicious nectar, insects often lose their foothold and plunge into the bottom of the narrow pitcher tube.

Once they fall, escape is impossible. The lower half of the pitcher tube is lined with long, needle-like hairs pointing downward to prevent the unfortunate insect from climbing up the wall. There is a pool of water at the bottom of the pitcher. The exhausted insect drowns in it and is digested.

A fly licking nectar, northern Alabama

Crawling insects follow the nectar trail on the outside of the pitcher and congregate on the pitcher opening where they find a lot of nectar. They walk around and feed on the delicious treat. But the ridge of the pitcher mouth is very slippery. They can also end up falling into the deep pitcher tube.

From the bottom of the pitcher, the blue sky looks bright. Any hope for freedom is fading for the unlucky bugs trapped in the pitcher — they are going to be dinner for the pitcher plant.

Hooded pitcher plant in Georgia

①

②

The moment of a fall

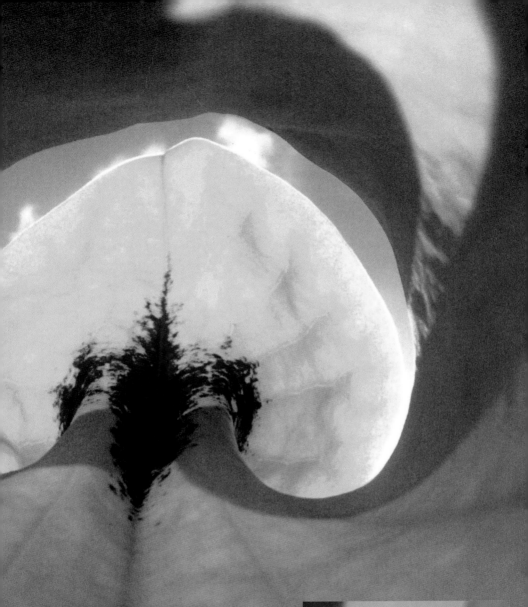

A bug's-eye view from
the bottom of a pitcher

Victims trapped in a pitcher

In northern California and southern Oregon, there grows a cousin of the pitcher plants, located many thousands of miles away from the savannas in the Southeast. Meet the cobra plant.

The cobra plant produces pitchers that stand two feet tall. The leaves twist about half a turn as they grow. The pitcher top is inflated like a dome that covers the pitcher mouth. A mustache-shaped projection grows from the edge of the mouth. This makes the leaf look like a deadly snake ready to attack. This gives the plant its name. Just like the pitcher plants in the Southeast, nectar attracts hungry insects to this pitfall trap.

Flying bugs land on the mustache to sip nectar and are gradually snared into the inflated dome because it looks invitingly bright. The dome ceiling has many small, white windows that confuse a bug into thinking there is an exit to the outside.

The insect may try to fly through, hit the
dome ceiling, and plummet into the deep

Cobra plant pitchers, Oregon

spiral tube. There is a small pool of water at the tube bottom. The prey drowns in it and eventually is digested by the plant. The cobra plant increases the amount of liquid in the pitcher when an insect is trapped.

Many white, worm-like creatures live in the pitcher liquid. Strangely, these tiny creatures are not eaten by the plant.

When insects fall into the pitcher and drown, these white worms attack the prey and rip them apart, so the cobra plant can break down the catch easily. What a nightmare for a trapped insect!

The cobra plant flowers in May. The blossoms are very colorful and mysterious-looking. The nodding flowers bloom on a tall stem nearly three feet high. The flowers resemble strange, *alien-like* faces.

What makes the flowers even more mysterious is that often spiders are found hiding inside the red flowers!

Cobra plant flowers, northern California

Chapter 5

Suction Trap

A nother type of insect-eating plant grows in the water, or in damp soil. They are bladderworts. We know there are at least 228 kinds of these plants in the world.

They have many tiny, balloon-like traps underwater. When a small water animal comes close to the trap and touches a trigger hair, the trap door suddenly opens, and the animal is sucked up into the trap along with the water. The door slams shut behind it and the prey is hopelessly imprisoned inside.

This happens in the blink of an eye — 1/30 of a second — the fastest movement among all plants.

Bladderwort flowers, Oregon

Purple-flowered bladderwort, in Georgia

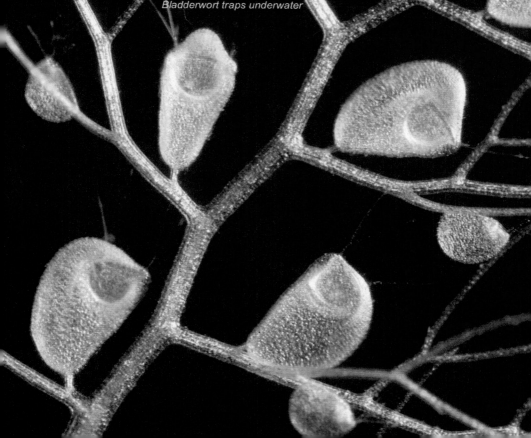

Bladderwort traps underwater

What is more amazing is that in less than half an hour, this miniature trap is reset automatically, and the trap is ready for another water worm to swim by. Traps are so good at catching bugs that oftentimes a single trap catches many water animals until it is completely full.

Prey capture ①

Prey capture ②

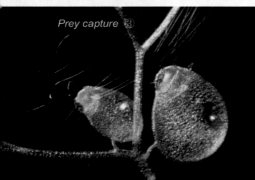
Prey capture ③

The captured animals are gradually broken down inside the trap. When this happens, the trap turns dark purple. The trap is the bladderwort's bug-eating stomach. The plant absorbs the nourishment from the trapped prey.

All the actions happen underwater

and the typical traps are very tiny. Even the largest one is about the size of the letter **O**.

So these plants are not very noticeable in the field, even if you happen to come across one — unless they are in flower. Their flowers are a beautiful bright yellow or purple, and often cover the entire pond or a large grassy field.

Yellow flowers of a terrestrial bladderwort, in Michigan

Chapter 6

*H*ow to Grow The

Carnivorous plants, in general, are delic plants and are typically found in bogs and other types of wetlands. Some carnivorous plants are endangered. The wild populations are shrinking because the land where they live has been cleared for homes and for other development.

You will be surprised to learn that Venus flytraps only grow wild in coastal North and South Carolina in the United States, and their number is declining. It is against the law to pick wild Venus flytraps.

Luckily, you can find many carnivorous plants in your local nurseries or nearby home centers. If you decide to grow them at home, the most important thing to remember is water, since they are bog plants. Keep the soil damp at all times. It is often a good idea to place a small tray of thin water under the flower pot. These plants are very sensitive to the water quality, so it may be wise to use pure drinking water. Keep the pot

Sparkling diamonds on a sundew leaf

in the windowsill, so the plants can receive bright sunlight at least part of the day. If you ever need to transplant the

Thread-leaf sundew and a spider

plants, use wet Sphagnum moss in place of regular soil. You can also try a soil mixture of half sand and half Sphagnum peat moss.

You may think that these meat-eating plants are always hungry. They are. But don't feed them hamburger — the plants will get indigestion and the leaf will turn black and wither. What they prefer is a fresh insect. If you manage to catch one, place it on the leaf.

Colorful pitchers

But don't overfeed the plants. They are perfectly OK without food for a long time. Besides, they often do catch bugs on their own without any help.

48

Made in the USA
Monee, IL
10 March 2021